Learning to Sail on Carlingford Lough

By

Peter O'Hare

ISBN: 978-1-913275-63-1

This book was published in cooperation with
Choice Publishing, Drogheda, Co. Louth,
Republic of Ireland.
www.choicepublishing.ie

Acknowledgements

Thanks to the editors of the following publications where
these poems were first published: *The New European:*
'Brexodus', 'Erasmus Mundus', 'Imperial Measures',
Independence Day', 'Learning to sail on Carlingford
Lough', ' The chapel of St. Patrick and the saints of
Ireland', 'The Last Harvest'. *Between the Lines (City Lit):*
'London Years', 'Prelude', 'Once', '800,000 Poppies'.

CONTENTS

Learning to sail on Carlingford Lough

London Years

Flights of Fancy

Dedication

To Patricia, for keeping the home fires burning.

Learning to sail on Carlingford Lough

Peter O'Hare

Learning to sail on Carlingford Lough

(Summer 1974)*

'Don't stray across the bow of the gunboat
just tack up-wind and leave it well astern',
a backstop that us Irish have to learn:
give lee-way to the Brits to stay afloat.
While drifting home across the darkening sea
not 'us' or 'them', it's just the breeze we tame
no gulf to cross, the tides remain the same
repeating their to and fro for centuries.

Above, the mountains play a waiting game
they've seen the Vikings and the Normans fail,
the winds don't sense a border or a pale
but mingle all together without shame,
both know we breathe the self-same air to live
and for everything we take something must give.

** The border between Northern Ireland and the Republic of
Ireland runs down the centre of Carlingford Lough. During 'The
Troubles' a Royal Navy vessel (known locally as the gunboat)
patrolled the lough.*

Haulbowline *

Poised between the realms of land and sea
a stalwart beacon from a surer time
the end-stop to a swollen borderline
among disputed eddies standing free.
Not where the continental shelf's cliff edge
meets the vastness of the abyssal plane
but subtly in darker shallows of pain
where only the flood tides expose the ledge.

Installed to curb the toll of precious lives
the oldest Irish rock lighthouse still stands
a symbol of resilience, it survives
among the grieving mountains of both lands.
A glowing glass still guiding from afar
the least treacherous way to cross the bar.

*Haulbowline lighthouse stands at the entrance to Carlingford
Lough where the border between Northern Ireland and the
Republic of Ireland ends.*

* * *

Narrow Water

Borne on the wings of hope, my father's hand
clasping at morsels in a lifeless hour
across the dark divide, that firm handshake
became the rock on which, one day, we'd build.

The smile that crossed a chasm in a blink
stirred the ancient bonds so long denied
the shared surrounds, the clouds, the gale force winds
the rugged hills that impinge upon the sky.

In mud and hope the cormorant still sits
observing coldly with his glassy eye, he knows,
though it cross the deepest fissure of the earth
a bridge is much more than just the shortest route.

Delivering puddings on Christmas Day

Apparently we'd always done it,
Dad quietly driving the old van,
down muddy boreens; to Minnie's Jimmy,
old Mrs.Coyle with her 90year old mother,
even the retired English lady, fallen on hard times.

It finally made sense: all the stirring of dried fruit,
bread-crumbs, the not-so-wee drop of whisky,
months back, in the pink plastic baby-bath, kept
for the purpose. Different-sized white porcelain bowls
tightly covered in foil, their cord ties neatly knotted.

If they had expected it, it didn't show.
"You're a wee angel" and truly I was.
I knew they were less fortunate, and rather odd,
but in those days we were all a bit odd,
in fact, it was a prerequisite, what made you
distinct,....valued.

Auntie Minnie's soda bread

Propped steaming precariously
against the cracked pane
on the sagging window ledge
of the wee pantry, wrapped
in a yellowing tea towel,
we could smell it
at the top of the stair.

By the creamy, half-empty
bottle of leftover buttermilk
we gobbled the sugared porridge
to be first to crumble
the soft, still-steaming dough
plastered with melting butter
and even more sugar.

Fortified for the shivering,
hour-long school bus ride
around the peninsula,
blinded by the winter sun-rise
glaring off the lough, and though
our puddle-wet toes froze
inside we were warmed.

Creamy, buttery, full-fat,
that's how we survived
those chilling winters
before the rule men
with their refrigeration
and their 'best before' dates
stymied Minnie's magic

We knew inside we were warm then
warmer than anyone in all of Cooley.

• • •

Rosary

The Luminous Mysteries hung in the air
once the silver and black marbled beads
were rescued from the back of the pantry drawer.

First, the Baptism of Jesus in the River Jordan,
then the Marriage Feast of Cana's ten Hail Mary's
rolled over Aunt Maureen's arthritic finger tips.

All five of us, on our knees, counting
on the cold, scrubbed kitchen floor,
me, hunched over granddad's chair.

The home-made woolly cushion,
balled from years of shiny trousers
smelling of pipe smoke, and the spittoon

in the corner, close to the old ceramic range
belching out little puffs of smoke
with every gust that rattled the widow frames.

The horse-shoe nailed above the door
for good fortune, and the spy-hole,
so Maureen could see who entered the shop.

She was always one step ahead,
but never led the rosary,
that was mum's job, keeping count,

herself a candle on dark October evenings.
'Wherever three or four are gathered in My name'
she would remind us 'God is there'.

And we felt it as we thumbed the beads,
our mumblings indecipherable to strangers,
sweeping us sleepwards ... binding us.

• • •

Refuge 1968

'There are people in the shore field, Daddy,
they'll be soaked and lashed by now'.
'Shush and help your mother
with buttering that bread,
we're feeding the five thousand
tonight, before you go to bed'

The rust blew off the Hillman van
as we drove the old shore road
rust and dust and soup flasks
green blankets from the press
and sliced pans stuffed with red cheese
in wax paper from McCanns.

I peered past the one loose wiper
as we lurched into our field, seeing
red haired women huddled around
a small gas stove with steaming broth,
pelted with hail and a raw east-wind
that had followed them south from Belfast.

'They've got nothing but the clothes
on their backs', said Aunty Maureen.
I only cared that Daddy was feeding
the five thousand and I was helping.
One old lady shivering in her pinny
grabbed a sandwich, 'God bless you, son'

Then one day they were gone,
but every July, for years, some came back.
There was one teary-eyed old man
gave us a crucifix made of lolly-sticks.
Maureen said it was from his son, a hunger striker,
we weren't quite sure where to put it.

• • •

Boy / Friend

To the Slate Rock
we ran, out-running
the wild, world-wind
that whisked us up-hill

unbound, silly
balls of energy
popping and hopping
across the crags

like billy goats, risking
the next slippery leap,
scuffed knees, dodging
the scratching gorse

sweating together
by the same streams
of spawning trout
as on we climbed

high up, we rounded
for the final stretch
to catch the three counties
in one wide sweep

and the Isle of Man.

We were the whole world then
before the fog
descended

like a papal cloak,
disorienting, dissembling,
clouding everything...

4.00 am

The flickering night-light
lengthens the shadows
on your bedroom wall

as twilight longings weave
their restless fidgetings
through twitching limbs,

disturbing the embered slumberings
of a passing world while
kindling a new dimension:

a land of constant dawn
where once lost opportunities
light the far horizons.

But your aging arms,
still hold on strong,
though the skin hangs looser now,

while that stubbornness
that stood in every doorway
hunts for its new home.

Footnote

It was there, hidden somewhere
amid the swollen ankles of the old ladies
who climbed the steep hill with you
to the chapel for the final time,
a last closeness, that ending need
to feel the passing of a parting friend.

Even the dark mountain bowed its head
like the village men walking sombrely
alongside, undaunted by the wet mist
that dampened all our shoulders
and clung as droplets to our best suits
yet held us all together as a moving mass.

Shuffling feet willing your transcendence
as if you were already lain beneath
the very paving stones on which we trod,
a parting gift, your final song
to remind us of how we belong
not what is fleeting, is going, or is gone.

Restoration

The whitewash flakes in my hand, his hand,
my breath leaves a bloom of mist on the lime,
retracing his every brush stroke as autumn light
illuminates my own age spots for the first time.

My eyes skim the same rough surface
resolving the limits of the crumbling render
layer after layer, outlining and guessing
reviving a life line, however slender.

'Je'es, I thought I'd seen your father's ghost,'
said gleam-eyed Jim, now hunched and small.
'It's the way you held the ladder, the angle of the brush
that cast the old man's shadow on the wall'.

'You know it was half-crazy all the things he did,
gilding the derelict shop-shutters and sills'
...I knew he'd painted the lamp posts in the village
I didn't know about the railings, the bin lids.

Veneration grows as more folk gather
recounting tales time won't eclipse,
their hope a tether as I sift and treasure
the pearls among the slaver from old men's lips.

How often had I passed that gable by
oblivious to my own ancestral call
hidden in the layers of soft brush strokes
mingled with his sweet breath on the wall.

Uncle Lauri

Without leaving a trace you taught me
how to loosen the halyard in a gale,
tether it with a bowline to the deck
tied with two half hitches, just to be safe.
When becalmed how to whistle for the wind,
and not to get tied in knots, but to know
how to keep my balance, while letting go
and still laugh together while shivering.

Then in winter, the warmth in your fingers
sealing the centreboard in the boat shed
without fuss, half-hidden, hardening me
to face the chills of the frostbite series,
so when the spinnaker tugged out I knew
I could surf up over the wave's crest, and fly.

Is the Pope Catholic ?

What kept compassion buried all those years
when empathy was such a by-passed word,
as God's own love was twisted to absurd
compulsions, cudgelled through contorted fears.
From centuries of pain the people spoke
reflecting on their depths of grief and shame
ensure those costs are never paid again
renew our scarred and wounded world with hope.

Throw open wide the gilded doors anew,
time to disinfect the crumbling spires
welcome and marry all, not just the few,
as one, dance down the aisles, combine the choirs.
Let God speak through the people once again,
their truth not mediated by old men.

Imperial Measures   *(...crossing the Irish border)*

The border crossed, ten miles become sixteen
when leaving Northern Ireland length extends
as one young country smiles at its new friends
the other still clings to its fading dream
when fond familiar forms were what it paid
for gains it once could certainly define
when even planets bowed to Greenwich time
the empire named in everything it weighed.

A guinea, shilling, farthing or a pinch
a perch, a rood, a gill; they still would rather
maintain ascendancy than shift an inch
off those lofty heights from which they barter.
Take heed before you lay the gauntlet down
better, for some, no bread than half a crown.

Grand Designs

What a beautiful room to die in
with its view of the trees and the sea
the plantation shutters lovingly worked
to outline the life of me.

What a beautiful room to pass in
as the sunrise creeps above the loch
it's blinding shimmer piercing the eye
cracking the hold of winter frosts.

What a beautiful wardrobe to die with
it's drawers built in at great expense
to hold all my ties and comforts
to be flogged from car boots when I'm gone.

And what perfect walls to gaze on
in my final, uncomfortable hours
my framed lighthouse poem, still assuring:
a beacon will keep glowing in the dark.

London Years

London Years

You see nothing but dull grime
and detest it.
I see sleaze and tease
and lap it up.
Spinning the appeal of its attractions;
better mettle and steel than Frankfurt.

We came in search of something,
to bring and leave,
and take and give.
Exchanged un-noticed gifts,
found wanting.
Moved to the suburbs, had the kids.

What happened to the London years?
Mods and Goths turned geeks and nerds.
I said 'let's make music'
You said 'feed the birds'.

Prelude

When that first note is launched into the glare
and humming violins return the call
my heart starts swelling with the rise and fall
and soon is swept along without a care.
A myriad of subtle voices dare
to intermingle just as they enthral
wrapping their sound around me like a shawl
its lulling, warming fibres made of air.

Yet in that very heat ferment the spores
that anguish, pain and tragedy still hide
like oceans tumult breaking on my shores
as riveted, I try to hold the tide
at bay, my life-long bolts no longer hold
as curtains rise my whole life's hurts foretold.

Opening Ceremony

Crammed into the wings, our nerves unfurled
on cue we strode like zealots for a cause
not just to win some medals or applause
but to share our wondrous city with the world.
Reclaiming centuries of toil and rust
from ruins of a green and pleasant land
we hauled almighty towers from the sand
and fired turbines with unspoken trust.

Such pride, we sensed the country felt it too
in our diversity we were complete,
but it was London, not England, that grew
before those left behind then stamped their feet.
Hope's not yet lost, you only have to delve
back to London in two thousand and twelve.

Return Mary Poppins !

Un-spun from the clouds on opening night
a flock of Mary Poppins' primly swooped,
all carpet bags and ankles, they induced
our unsuspecting hearts' nostalgic flight.
The groundswell of a memory's brief rebirth
transfixed our flabbergasted gaze and tamed
our sky-struck eyes. Sheer awe could not be feigned;
that day it was the greatest show on earth.

Umbrellas floating down the evening breeze
confirmed that fairy tales could still come true
glide north above the shires and the trees
melt all those hardened hearts to feel it too.
A new spoonful of sugar might yet show
they've not all gone where the lost hearts go.

Independence Day

Let's wrest control again I hear you say
and stamp our own two feet upon the world
until the towers shake, their flags unfurled,
the beggars squeezed until they've paid their way.
Bring back the steelworks from away back when
we ruled the waves and bound slaves to our plan.
Rebuild the greatest follies known to man
and make the 'great' in Britain grate again.

Forget the huddled masses at our shore
let Greeks and Turks and Swedes decide their fate.
Once more unto the breach to bolt the door
before the swamp's brim-filled and it's too late.
For when the plague subsides we'll go no more
to Rome, but cower behind our garden gate.

Il Viaggio a Reims

It happened too in eighteen twenty five
when Europe's great were called to congregate,
Rossini charged to celebrate the fete:
his great subversive opera came alive.
Unheard by Brits till nineteen ninety two
when mistaken as an apt collusion
for London's presidency of the Union
to show how European we were too.

How trite this island's efforts on that day
our continental kinship to acclaim,
on stage the singers also lost their way
awaiting carriages that never came.
How fitting; hitting all the notes in vain,
must Europe's cognoscenti laugh again?

Hovercraft

Gliding sideways on silver-gilded seas
with rubber skirts trapping hot air beneath
it's Rolls Royce engine whirring on a sheath
a miracle of motion and of ease.
One cocksure captain rallying his team
to seize the brash attention that he craves
and sate his on-going need to rule the waves
from rusting scrapyard remnants of a dream.
We're not those old inventors in their sheds
for whom it was their last, their final page
once feted, now embarrassing instead
detritus of a once great golden age.
Instead, blown way off course by wind and tide
hold tight, it's going to be a bumpy ride.

English fog

Has London's landscape languished over time
since Monet and Pissarro first laid eyes
on Upper Norwood's hills and cloudy skies,
the smog-bound city where their art would shine?
The fog has lifted from the river's edge
and gleaming towers now replace the old,
but first impressions can retain their hold
though stubborn minds still seek to drive a wedge.

An island insularity remains,
the push and tug of closeness pulled apart
in spite of Brexiteers outlandish claims
this city still craves commerce over art.
Redemption may require but a twist:
be French to really see the English mist.

Brexodus

Beguiling glimmers of fortune drew us
to this island gifting a generous life.
Before brash nativism became rife
we felt accepted by those who knew us.
But some had patently reached their limit
turning their backs, though we had toiled so hard.
It wasn't that casual disregard
but the cold condescension that did it.

So now we are leaving with heavy hearts
where is the fabled graciousness you claim,
all we were seeking was a bright new start
not to endure imperial disdain.
We leave this country much poorer for sure;
let the empire's sons now heave the manure.

Island Britain

Elgar's enigma on Sunday morning
gardener's question-time on radio four
pink roses, deftly pruned by the front door
before afternoon tea on parquet flooring.
But Cornish fishermen sense the foreboding
as Atlantic mists roll in on Poldark's moor
and plaintive highland bag-pipes grieve before
Anglesea registers the gale warning.

Innocent youngsters swept up by the flood
once fellow-citizens of everywhere,
stunned by complicity, they sit and stare
watching the brambles take over the wood.
Scanning their Facebook feeds, tears in their eyes,
the cheated generation learns to cry.

The chapel of St. Patrick and the saints of Ireland
Westminster Cathedral, 11 November 2019

Obscured by a Byzantine colonnade
with polished shamrocks of the darkest greens
an English travesty of Irish dreams
a frozen tribute to a past charade.
Bonds between Kings and countries, gods and men
annulled by decades of unanswered prayer,
still unrequited kinship stalks the air
a fathomless gulf between us and them.

The innocence of youth once forced to reap
an unsought purgatory on foreign shores,
a century is long enough to weep
for futile trust that did not end all wars.
The empire's dead, reclaim again as ours
the god of oceans, cliffs and glistening stars.

800,000 poppies

The impact gasp
widened the eye
and shell-shocked the heart.

A blood-red carpet
still, yet moving.
Shimmering from a distance,

Ill-fitting close-up,
silk-like ceramic petals
actually hard as gun-shot.

100 years of answers
still unquestioned, now
malletted into the soft moat.

Protected by steel toe-caps
I hammer home:
number 757,263.

carefully placed,
not overlapping,
just touching.

The day freedom-of-movement died

I found myself, checking
the expiry date on a packet
of *Taste the Difference* Belgian waffles
on a shelf in Sainsburys, just in case.
Then wandered along Westow Street
past the Greek Orthodox Church
and caught a glimpse of a golden icon
catching the sun through a side door.
'*Mi cocina es tuya*' implored
the near-empty Venezuelan restaurant,
next door, Bambos, the Cypriot barber
propping up the doorway, smiled
his seemingly permanent smile.
I passed the Polish foodstore, krupnioki
in the window, slowing down outside
the Cafe St. Germain as the whiff
of croissants filled the air, then hovered
outside Lorenzo's Espresso bar
before opting for the Portuguese cafe
for Nadia and Augustino's sumptuous
Pastel de Nata. Remembering
on the way home, not to forget
fresh garlic from the Turkish corner shop
next to the Kurdish kebab house
as out of nowhere a hailstorm
pelted the pavement, I rummaged
desperately in my bag, soaked to the skin,
all the umbrellas of Cherbourg
fading in the distance.

The Last Harvest

As if to warn of harsh dark hours to come
the sun colludes with nature to provide
bounteous boughs of apple, pear and plum
splurging it's lush abundance far and wide.
The warmest summer in a hundred years
leaves Europe basking but just tears my heart,
conflicting omens feed my looming fears,
the comfort of consensus prised apart.

Where have the kind hands gone that reaped the fruit?
the quiet men who toiled from dawn to dark
the silent fields that once absorbed their youth
now haunted by their shadows, long and stark.
Too late to quell, festering in the rough,
the guilt of not being vigilant enough.

The English Variant

Mutated on the coat-tails of empire
left with a boastful shell, a hardened crust
immune to logic argument, it's thrust
is as lethal as a deceitful liar.
Inbred, so not transmissible, as such,
nor brought from foreign shores or escapades
passed down through ceremonies and parades
it's attributes a talisman, a crutch.
Patterned on playing fields of punishment
impairing it's potential to take stock,
with scarcely concealed astonishment
it cares nothing about its aftershock.
The world waits for a vaccine to wrench apart
the rusted scaffolding that holds its heart.

Quadruple By-pass
(King's College Hospital, London, February 2018)

This must be what dying feels like:
numbness everywhere
but where it hurts.

The essence disconnected,
re-assembled sections
searching for the pulse,

struggling for sense
and feeling,
in a blind alley.

'Hello, I'm Clodagh, from Cork,
and I'm your nurse for today.
What would you like for breakfast ?',

...then all the long gone Irish breezes
the memories of warm scones,
the comforting soups, rekindle.

All the mother's milk that ever flowed,
tumbles out, and gushes
from a deep well.

Despite the tilting of the planet,
the severed tributaries
find their way back to the ocean

and I can still cry.

● ● ●
33

Sylvan Hill

I climbed the hill I hadn't climbed in years
and breathed the freshest air I could recall
on London's southern slopes, no haze at all,
just trills of native birds teasing my ears.
When forced by shared concern to hold our breath
the whole world seemed to stop and look around
the wonder on our doorstep now re-found,
a one-time reminder of natures wealth.
Can it have been so easy all this time?
why did we have to wait for such a cue
to force us to slow up and sense the rhyme,
deep down we surely know what we must do.
Don't start the planes or fly south to Peru
just climb a hill to paint the sky more blue.

Dusk

If she could hold the solace of the sun
the bright all-seeing conscience of the moon
she'd light the ancient texts on gravestones hewn
that warn safeguarding sense is never done.
If even ancient Greeks could go astray
then common wealth can easily implode,
without so much as forking in the road
she frets at how old England's lost its way.

The aged dowager, pacing the halls
assuming all the duties are assigned,
still haughty, though dementia's shadow falls,
she wonders why the brasses still aren't shined.
Keep standing tall, adjust the slipping crown
bewildered as you watch the sun go down.

Flights of Fancy

Once

Once, might be a fleeting fancy
a wild spree in an open car.
Once, might be a slip that leaves
a mutilating life-long scar.

Once, might be a fatal jump
a cliff-edge leap with no way back.
Once, might be a foolish turn
a dead-end off the garden path.

Once, might be a golden try-out
the final chance to join the team.
Once, might be a lonely step
the last gasp of a long held dream.

Till you, whose eyes shone with such lust
that I too, craved and hoped could be
the start of a dark obsession, but no,
once meant nothing more than ....once

Slow Foxtrot

I used to know what was me
and what was yours, not mine,

but they sought each other in our dance
lulled by rhythms long and close

'till fusing fibres soldered firm
by trust and hope moved us as one.

Though long since perished, cracked and gone
they left defined how fine a line

lies between 'almost' and 'forever',
you and me, your time and mine.

This small life

Your kernel knew,
as we did not
the consequence
of Fall

Hope's berries
flush yet compassing,
death's distance
and his call.

Once that friend
reaper, fertilised
your elemental
song

Your poets summer
shared its promise
circumferenced,
'small'.

Concorde

Thrilled by the craft and elegance of flight
two old antagonists, their strengths combined,
soared above the turbulence of the time
and wrought a masterpiece of pure delight.
Launched in perfect form at its eager birth
a sleek embodiment of the sublime,
a dream that broke the grip of space and time
to follow the curvature of the earth.

Why leave the first class lounge and so discard
the finest claret, served on board, to kings
why tramp the whole world seeking such regard
with silver service waiting in the wings.
A finer flourishing could not be found:
to sip champagne at twice the speed of sound.

Damnatio Memoriae

The great betrayals live long in the soul
of brotherhoods who've had to fight to breathe,
leaving new generations to reprise
the unsung lamentations of the old.
No matter how survivors tear them down
our leaders callous deeds are not erased
the decent family men we seldom praise
but the Nero's and Caligula's we crown.
How much of air and time must they command
before their icons fade, their statues fall,
are we doomed, like our forebears on this land,
too charmed to really see what they stand for:
a wanton drive to carve their names in stone
regardless for what crimes they may be known.

Erasmus Mundus

Would wise Erasmus shiver in his grave
watching the twists and turns of Europe's course?
No doubt he'd hide a smile, sensing the source,
knowing the path corrupting scribes can pave.
Although five hundred years have come and gone
the evidence of lessons learned is slight
great slaughter has not curbed the urge to fight,
among the blind the one-eyed men rule on.
But scholarships of sharing can still heal
and help young minds to blossom, fresh and new
observe and learn from others how their zeal
can urge to aid the many, not the few,
and see with youth's clear eyes, while still in thrall,
this world; the common sanctuary of all.

Song of Nineveh

The oldest notes of music set in stone
survive beneath our feet to sing again;
"Ashurbanipal lives, King of all men
through whom the God's loving power is shown."
He stored all the known wisdom of the earth,
inscriptions in clay since before the flood,
his aqueducts flushed apricots to bud
winged lions proclaimed his cultures rebirth.

Droughts and wars, millennia have passed, yet
the fingers on the walls look like our own.
Unearthed in time to come, by youthful sweat,
who will read from *our* long abandoned stones
that art, music and power were combined
to bring peace and harmony to humankind?

Too Late

The saddest phrase in any spoken tongue
when most tragic mistakes are realised
like songbirds hunted down on distant isles
their glorious chords forever left unsung.
As hubris stumbles towards a final act
its farcical plot-twists unravelling
in open view, though those still challenging
care not about the evidence they lack.

What hope of yet another song filled dawn?
of rebuilt compromise and lasting trust
the old alliance on the White House lawn
when 'bi-partisan' really did mean all of us.
Some pray for the lost songbirds return, and wait,
alas, the history books may cry: "Too Late".

Inhumation

Again, a blast
has vaporised
humanity

Except for me,
trying out the latest
heavy lead coffin
in the basement.
It fits perfectly.
I especially like
the simple,
modern lines.
Heaving off
the solid lid
a profound
absence
reminds me
of how bored
death must be